Media and

W9-CTI-280

ADVERTISING

CENSORSHIP

LAWRENCE SOLEY

The Southshore Press
Milwaukee

Studies of advertising censorship by Lawrence Soley, on which this report draws, were published originally in *Journal of Advertising*, *Extra!*, and *Censorship, Inc.*

A Southshore Press First Edition.

Library of Congress Cataloging-in-Publication Data

Soley, Lawrence.
     Advertising Censorship / Lawrence Soley.
     p. cm. -- Media and Business Studies Series
     ISBN 0-9720516-0-0
     1. Communication - Economic aspects
     2. Corporations - United States

Page and cover design by Theresa.

9 8 7 6 5 4 3 2 1

Printed in the U.S.A.

The television sponsor... has
reached the ultimate status:
most decision-making swirls
at levels below him, requiring
only his occasional benediction
at this or that selected point.
He is a potentate of our time.

Erik Barnouw
(1908-2001)

In *Freedom of the Press*, reporter and press critic George Seldes (1935) charged that advertisers, not government, were the principal news censors in the United States. Seldes reported that advertisers often pressured newspapers to kill or alter stories about their businesses or personnel, and newspapers also censored stories out of deference "toward the sources of their money" without having been pressured. According to Seldes, the "suppression of news by department stores [*the largest advertisers at the time*] is the most frequent and flagrant story" (pp. 42, 43).

Newspapers and other media edit or kill stories offensive to advertisers because media profits come from the sale of advertising, not sales of the medium to consumers. With newspapers and magazines, subscription and single copy sales typically account for less than 25 percent of gross revenues; profit comes from advertising (Willis, 1988; Norris, 1982). With electronic media -- except for noncommercial and pay services such as HBO and Showtime that do not carry advertising -- almost all of the revenues and profits are derived from advertising.

Seldes (1935) recounts numerous instances where advertisers succeeded in suppressing news during the 1930s. For example, news about a rape case where the son of a Philadelphia department store owner was the defendant was suppressed in every newspaper in that city, apparently at the request of the father. Seldes (1935) reports that in July 1932, Procter & Gamble cancelled its advertising in newspapers that carried a syndicated article telling readers how to make soap at home. These are examples of direct censorship, where advertisers pressure media to change or kill stories or punish media for their reporting by withdrawing advertising.

Direct advertiser pressure still exists. *The Duluth News Tribune*, the only daily newspaper in the city of Duluth, Minnesota, responded to threats from real estate advertisers by firing a columnist who wrote a "Smart Shopper" column describing how homeowners could sell their homes themselves. The newspaper also gave the executive vice-president of the Minnesota Association of Realtors, whose members purchase a large percentage of the newspaper's advertising, space to reply to the column, and the newspaper's editor wrote an editorial criticizing the columnist for being "contradictory... incomplete... and unfair." In response, the columnist filed a libel suit against the newspaper (Grow, 1992).

However, advertising censorship is usually not as direct or heavy-handed as this. As Seldes (1935) pointed out, media often kill stories out of deference "toward the sources of their money" without being asked. For example, the *New York World*, one of the most prestigious newspapers of the 1930s, refused to publish an O. Henry story about an underpaid department store employee who was willing to sacrifice "her virtue." The *World* refused the story out of fear that it would "harm its relations with all department stores" (Seldes, 1935, p. 43). This is an example of self-censorship, which also still occurs. A more recent example is the killing of a story about Carnival Cruise lines in a New York City daily. After protesters criticized Kathy Lee Gifford and her clothing line for exploiting child laborers in Asia, a reporter decided to do a story on the working conditions on Carnival Cruise ships, for which Gifford was spokesperson. The travel editor heard about the story and killed it, saying that story would cost the paper lucrative cruise ship advertising (Fleetwood, 1999). When a story about an airline crash was "uncomfortably close" to an airline advertisement at the *Wisconsin State Journal*, the story was killed (Cooper, 1993). After the *Columbia Journalism Review* publicized the incident, criticizing the newspaper, editor Frank Denton defended the action, claiming the copy editor had killed "an insignificant, disposable brief about a minor overseas plane crash rather than let the compositor rearrange ads and remake pages" (Denton, 1993).

Media can also bury a story to appease advertisers. Burying a story means that the story is run, but is given less prominence than it deserves. A buried story can be moved from the front page to the business section, reduced to a paragraph or two, or edited so that potentially offensive content appears at the end of the article, where few readers will see it. For example, a *New York Times* story by reporter Blake Fleetwood (1999) examined how the Tiffany jewelry store on Fifth Avenue, one of the *Times'*s most consistent advertisers, received a $4.5 million tax break from a state program designed to keep businesses from moving out-of-state. Although the story appeared on page one of the newspaper, it was rewritten with the discussion of Tiffany in the 19th paragraph.

During the decades following publication of *Freedom of the Press*, numerous examples of how advertisers have influenced the content of news and entertainment shows surfaced. In 1948, Jack Benny was asked by radio commentator Walter Winchell to plug on his show one of Winchell's favorite causes - - the Damon Runyon Cancer Center. Although Benny attended a fund raiser for the Center, he refused to mention it on his show. He informed Winchell that because "I am sponsored by a cigarette maker, we are not permitted at any time to mention the word cancer" (Laurance, 1999, p. E6). Another cigarette company prohibited mention of the word "parliament," even when referring to the British legislative body, because it was the name of a competing cigarette brand. Camel cigarettes also prohibited shows that it sponsored from naming characters "Lucky," the brand name of its chief competitor; banned the showing of "no smoking" signs in sponsored programs; and discouraged showing famous people, except Winston Churchill, smoking cigars. These rules even applied to newscasts, such as the *Camel News Caravan* (Barnouw, 1978; Bagdikian, 1995). Similarly, when *Playhouse 90* staged a docudrama on the Nuremburg trials, CBS prohibited use of the word "gas chambers" because the show's sponsor was a gas company (Laurance, 1999).

Even the infamous quiz scandals of the 1950s were due to advertising pressures. Charles Revlon, owner of the cosmetic company that sponsored the *$64,000 Question*, "had repeatedly given orders as to which contestants should win -- and thus continue on the series -- and which should be disposed of. He left details to the producers, but was furious if his instructions were not carried out" (Barnouw, 1978, p. 56).

Television was not the only medium muscled by advertisers in the post-World War II era. In 1954, General Motors withdrew its advertising from the *Wall Street Journal* because the newspaper refused to accept the release dates set by GM on stories about its new models (Banks, 1978).

Albert N. Halverstadt, the advertising manager for Procter & Gamble, the country's largest advertiser, testified in 1965 that his company had policies prohibiting its advertisements from appearing in programs that do not "minimize the 'horror' aspects" of war, depict men in uniform as villains, or cast business "as cold, ruthless and lacking all sentiment or spiritual motivation" (Bagdikian, 1995). Without advertising from large firms such as Procter & Gamble, programs with this content were never produced.

Procter & Gamble still prohibits its ads from appearing in controversial television programs. In 2001, Procter & Gamble cancelled scheduled commercials in an episode of "Family Law" dealing with a child-custody case that showed the mother owning a gun. Although

CBS found advertisers to buy the cancelled time at the last moment, the network cancelled the summer rerun of the episode rather than having to search for substitute advertisers (Ostrow, 2001).

There are numerous examples of advertisers pressuring mass media to kill or alter stories during the 1970s and 1980s. The New York Times Company was forced to sell *Modern Medicine* magazine to Harcourt Brace Jovanovich in 1976 after pharmaceutical firms threatened to withdraw their advertising. The threat was made because the *New York Times* newspaper published articles on medical malpractice that angered the pharmaceutical industry. Since these firms didn't advertise in, and therefore couldn't punish the newspaper, they threatened the Times Corp.-owned magazine (Bagdikian, 1995). During the same period, Braniff Airways, First National Bank of Chicago, Westinghouse and other corporations cancelled their advertising in *Business Week* after the magazine upset the companies by its reporting (Banks, 1978).

A decade later, the *Los Angeles Herald Examiner* published an investigative report about Southern California grocery stores' shortweighting and overcharging customers. "Ralphs, one of the region's largest supermarket chains, responded by canceling its $250,000 advertising contract with the paper. Although the report caused the Los Angeles county board of supervisors to launch an investigation of supermarket pricing practices, the *Los Angeles Times* never picked up the story" (Mencher, 1986).

Similar pressures are exerted on weekly newspapers,

which are far more dependent on advertising revenues from a small group of businesses than daily newspapers. In Iowa, Pottsville State Bank withdrew its advertising from the *Pottsville Herald* after the weekly carried an Associated Press report stating that the bank had one of Iowa's lowest ratios of loans to assets. The bank never advertised in the paper again, and even helped form a "community improvement committee" that drove the *Herald* out of business (Nauer and Rhodes, 1992).

The Valley Star in Velva, North Dakota faced a similar boycott in 1999. Alarmed by the paper's investigative stories, such as one about the city auditor using her public office to run a real estate business, members of Velva Association of Commerce launched an advertising boycott of the paper. The city bank, the local electric utility and other businesses boycotted the paper, hoping to shut it down. Businessman Dan Craig, a commerce association member, said that he withdrew his advertising because the "the paper needs to be more positive rather than scrutinizing every little thing a community does" (Donovan, 1999).

Advertising pressure is even exerted on alternative media, which pride themselves as modern-day muckrakers. Nemer, Fieger and Associates, Inc., which buys three-fourths of the motion picture advertising in the Twin Cities, withdrew its ads from the *Twin Cities Reader* because it was angered by a column describing that year's crop of movies as bores (Marcotty, 1992). In Detroit, the *Metro Times* conducted an investigation of the strong arm methods used by record chains against small retailers selling used CDs. After receiving ad boycott threats from record companies, the paper dropped the story (Fleetwood, 1999).

Publisher Gloria Steinem (1990) described some of the advertiser pressures on *Ms.* magazine before it went adless in 1990. Clairol withdrew its advertising from *Ms.* after the magazine briefly mentioned a congressional inquiry into the possibility that hair dying chemicals were carcinogenic. Procter & Gamble, which has repeatedly influenced media content, attempted to restrict reportage by writing into advertising contracts stipulations about editorial content. According to Steinem, Procter & Gamble prohibits its products from being advertised "in any issue that included any material on gun control, abortion, the occult, cults or the disparagement of religion." Caution was also demanded in any issue covering sex or drugs, even for educational purposes. Another example of how advertisers pressured *Ms.* occurred when the magazine pictured dissident Soviet women without makeup on its cover: Revlon decided not to advertise in the magazine.

Print media -- newspapers and magazines -- are not the only media pressured by advertisers. Many television and radio stations have also been pressured by advertisers to kill or alter news stories. In Los Angeles, veteran consumer reporter David Horowitz was let go in 1996 from KCBS-TV, a CBS owned-and-operated station, after automobile advertisers repeatedly complained to management about his stories on car safety. According to Horowitz, management had first tried to stop his investigations with comments such as, "I'm concerned about the story not because it's right or wrong, but it may cost us advertising" (Kurtz, 1996; Mink, 1996). As this example illustrates, working for a large, corporate-owned station like CBS doesn't mean that reporters will be protected from advertising censorship.

Some defenders of advertising – mostly professors who teach advertising and marketing – deny that advertisers pressure the news media, despite the ample anecdotal evidence. For example, marketing professors Rot-feld and Lacher (1994) report that "newspaper publishers' concerns for offending advertisers are tied to other concerns for the general reading audience. They wish to avoid offending advertisers in the same fashion that they do not wish to offend readers, knowing that both are necessary for the publication's success. But this is not unethical control or influence by advertisers" (p. 4).

Advertising, Its Role in Modern Marketing, a college text written by four advertising professors, reports that "some reason exists to believe that small, financially insecure newspapers or broadcast stations are more likely to be influenced by outside pressure than the large, financially stable ones. There is little reason to believe that large, prestigious papers, magazines, or television networks... cater particularly to advertisers, as charged by critics" (Krugman, et. al., 1994, p. 93). The text dismisses the many reports of advertising pressure by suggesting that there "are certain built-in checks against advertisers exerting too much influence on the media. Perhaps the strongest check is the self-interest of media executives. They cannot afford to ignore news of interest to readers, listeners, or viewers and expect to retain public confidence.... We suspect that the media are probably much less 'kept' than most people think. He who pays the piper does not necessarily call the tune," the text concludes (p. 93).

Not only does evidence contradict this assertion, but there is also evidence that the mass media provide positive coverage for advertisers, and this practice is quite old. In her memoir, *The Girls in the Balcony*, former *New York Times* reporter Nan Robertson revealed that writers for the women's page were required to do positive stories about *Times* advertisers in the 1950s. She wrote that "every fashion writer was assigned a group of department and specialty stores. We were required to come up every month with articles whose column-inches reflected the relative advertising strength of every store.... The monitor of all this was Monroe Green, the advertising director of *The New York Times*, who had been a powerful executive for many years at Macy's. There was hell to pay from Green every time an advertiser was not adequately represented in the 'news' columns of the women's page" (Robertson, 1992, pp. 82-83).

This practice hasn't stopped. The *Greensboro News & Record* devoted half its November 30, 1997 front page and an additional 48 column inches on page four to a story about holiday shopping. The article mentioned the newly-opened Target department store 14 times and an additional three times in captions under photos taken at Target (Cooper, 1998). The *Detroit News* and the *Detroit Free Press* published numerous stories, photos and sidebars about the Somerset North shopping mall that opened in 1997, including two full-color sections with copy.

On the front pages, the papers announced that more information about the mall was available on their websites (Cooper, 1997). The Albany *Times Union* ran a front page announcement on July 10, 1998 describing Delta Airline's new service to Orlando. The announcement included information on routes and fares, red and white Delta logos, and even a color photo of a Delta executive. The "news" story mentioned Delta 22 times (Cooper, 1999). Target, mall stores, and the airline were advertisers in the newspapers.

Some newspaper executives openly admit that newspaper stories promote advertisers. *Chicago Sun Times* executive editor Larry Green said this about plugging advertisers: "We have to take care of our customers" (Fleetwood, 1999).

ADVERTISING PRESSURES ON NEWSPAPERS

Of the major media, daily newspapers should be the least susceptible to advertiser pressures because most dailies are monopolies. In the vast majority of U.S. cities, there is only one daily newspaper. In just a few dozen of the largest cities, such as New York, Boston and Chicago, are there competing newspapers. In most cities with two dailies, such as San Francisco, Seattle and Detroit, the dailies do not compete directly for advertising because they are either co-owned — that is, owned by one publisher — or are published under the Newspaper Preservation Act. The Newspaper Preservation Act allows "competing" newspapers to share an advertising department and printing plant, but requires the papers to maintain separate news departments. As a consequence, jointly-published newspapers do not compete for advertising: Advertisers are often sold space in both newspapers or pay a hefty premium to advertise in just one. For example, the *Detroit News* and *Detroit Free Press* charge advertisers $537 per column inch when both papers are purchased. If an advertiser wants to buy just one newspaper, the rate is $483 per column inch (Standard Rate and Data Service, 1999, p. 308). Clearly, the rates strongly encourage advertisers to buy advertising in both.

In addition, there has been consolidation in the newspaper industry with large chains such as Gannett, Knight Ridder, Ingersoll, Scripps-Howard and the New York Times corporations buying up and owning more newspapers today than ever. These large companies and their newspapers should be less susceptible to advertiser pressure than small, independent newspaper publishers, as the authors of *Advertising, Its Role in Modern Marketing* (1994) suggest. Large media corporations are not as dependent on a few advertisers as are small independent newspapers, and the largeness of the companies should insulate their papers from pressure applied by local advertisers.

Despite the theory, there is overwhelming evidence showing that advertisers pressure newspapers to kill or change news stories, and that many large and small newspapers have caved in to the pressure. The most pressure comes from two industries -- real estate and automobile -- that are the first and third heaviest advertisers in newspapers. (Department stores are the second heaviest advertisers.) For example, U.S. auto dealers spent a record $5.3 billion on advertising in 1998, four percent more than in 1997, and over half went to newspapers (Associated Press, 1999). For their money, auto dealers expect to get favorable coverage or will withdraw their advertising from newspapers. As Leon Edward of Edwards Chevrolet in Birmingham, Alabama, former president of the National Automobile Dealer Association, said, "Dealers have the right to spend money where they want to spend it. If somebody is giving you a black eye, it is hard to spend money with them" (Lawrence, 1995, p. 8).

The pressure from automobile dealers was described in a *Washington Journalism Review* article titled, "Auto Dealers Muscle the Newsroom" (Singer, 1992). The article provides some examples of the types of pressure applied by auto dealers. When the *Daily Spectrum* in St. George, Utah published a syndicated article telling readers how to bargain for new cars, area auto dealers withdrew their advertising from the paper. Under pressure from the dealers, the paper published a retraction, claiming that the article was run because of an editor's "poor judgement." After the *Manchester Herald* ran the same article, the editor responsible was sacked. And when the *Hartford Courant*, owned by the giant Times Mirror Corp., carried a story describing the high-pressure sales tactics used by some area auto dealers during a "Presidents Weekend" sales blitz, some dealers pulled their advertising from the paper. The publisher apologized to these dealers in a letter, pointing out that there "were several other stories that were either 'positive' or thoughtful accounts" of auto dealers in the paper that weekend.

After Bruce Wissinger of the Johnstown, Pennsylvania *Tribune-Democrat* wrote a tongue-in-cheek column about his car-buying experiences, twenty automobile dealers cancelled their newspaper advertising. In an effort to bring the auto dealers back, advertising manager Brian Long sent a letter to the dealers condemning Wissinger's "misguided" column. The letter failed to appease the auto dealers, most of whom continued their ad boycott for months (Giobbe, 1994).

The advertising pressure was so intense on Forum Communications, the owner of newspapers and broadcast stations in the upper Midwest, that it banned consumer reports about automobiles after auto dealers conducted a costly, year-long boycott of the North Dakota *Fargo Forum* (Fleetwood, 1999).

After the San Jose *Mercury News*, the flagship paper of the Knight Ridder Corp., ran an article headlined, "A Car Buyer's Guide to Sanity," which told readers how to negotiate lower prices, area auto dealers became enraged and demanded a meeting with the paper's publisher, Jay T. Harris. Harris met with the dealers, apologized, and offered them a free full-page of advertising to make up for the story, but was unable to lessen their anger. After meeting with Harris, the dealers — members of the Santa Clara County Motor Dealers Association — met in a nearby hotel, where they decided to collectively withdraw their adverting from the paper. The action cost the *Mercury News* $1 million in revenue and attracted the attention of the Federal Trade Commission (FTC), which issued a complaint against the association and its members, asserting that the collective boycott violated federal antitrust laws (Kurtz, 1996; Chiuy, 1995).

The Santa Clara County Motor Dealers Association settled the FTC complaint in 1995, agreeing to avoid advertising boycotts in the future, amending the association's bylaws to include the federal restriction, and educating member auto dealers about the terms of the settlement. Although settling the suit, the Association maintained that it had done nothing wrong.

The FTC acted because the dealers' collusion deprived consumers of price information contained in ads and "was designed to chill the publication from publishing similar stories in the future," explained FTC official Mark Whitener at the time of the settlement. The boycott therefore constituted an unlawful restraint of trade. FTC officials also pointed out that the settlement did not prohibit individual car dealers from boycotting a newspaper; it merely prohibited collective boycotts (Gilje, 1995; Ramirez, 1995).

The settlement, and the ensuing publicity that it garnered, has reduced the number of group boycotts initiated by car dealers, but it has not stopped individual car dealers from pulling their ads. Nor has it stopped newsrooms from fearing auto dealer pressures.

Another tactic used by newspapers to appease auto dealers has been to move the automotive section from the news department to the advertising department. *The Birmingham News* created the "Wheels" section to appease advertisers. It was created because "we were losing automotive advertising," reported section manager Dennis Washburn to the *Washington Journalism Review*.

ADVERTISING CENSORSHIP   19

"Our editorial people began writing some very critical stories.... We lost two major advertisers -- $300,000 to $500,000 a year -- right here. Then we started the 'Wheels' section," which Washburn says is "designed to sell cars" (Singer ,1992, p. 16).

The Birmingham News isn't the only newspaper that created an advertorial section to appease auto dealers. *The Milwaukee Journal-Sentinel*, a monopoly newspaper, turned its "Transportation" section over to the Automobile Dealers Association of Mega Milwaukee (ADAMM). ADAMM writes the articles for the section, which has the appearance of being a regular section of the newspaper. However, the section carries advertorials with headlines such as "Cadillac DTS Sedan Debuts as Showcase for High-tech Hardware" and "Infiniti 130 Sedan Mixes Strong Engine with Plush Comforts" (*Milwaukee Journal Sentinel,* 1999).

Real estate brokers and builders also throw their advertising weight around the newsroom, as the "Smart Shopper" columnist for *The Duluth News Tribune* learned. And the pressure is common. In a 1991 survey of real estate editors, 44 percent reported that publishers or senior editors prohibit the real estate section from carrying balanced news for fear of angering advertisers. Instead, the editors produced industry-friendly copy. The publisher and senior editors' fears are not imagined, either: More than 80 percent of the real estate editors said advertisers had threatened to cancel their advertising because of a news story (Swallow Williams, 1991).

One survey respondent reported that nearly every real estate agent in town complained after the newspaper carried a story about selling a home without a broker. "The result is that now we only run fluff." Another reported that the "publisher once stopped the press run of the section when he saw a wire story critical of real estate agents." Another reported that a story about slumping condominium sales angered condo brokers, who complained that the coverage was going to make sales worse. Several large advertisers cancelled their advertising in protest.

The experiences of *The Islander*, a small circulation newspaper on Edisto Island, South Carolina, are illustrative of the problems that papers can face when they anger the real estate and building industries. The newspaper ran a front page story based on a Duke University report commissioned by the Edisto Beach Property Owners Association which concluded that the best method for dealing with beach erosion was to stop rebuilding houses that had been washed away. The story, which was accompanied by a satiric illustration of a postcard reading, "Greetings from Beautiful Erosion City," led to a boycott, which caused advertising to drop by 50 percent. One real estate agent was so angered by the story that he drove around town gathering up the newspaper's orange street boxes, which he dumped on the porch of the newspaper office (McInerney, 1994).

Larger circulation newspapers have also been pressured by realtors. Some, including the Fort Lauderdale *Sun Sentinel* and Boca Raton *News*, have their advertising or marketing departments produce the real estate section, as is done with some automotive sections, to relieve the pressure (Lesly, 1991).

Newspapers are pressured by other large advertisers, not just auto dealers and real estate brokers. Department stores, airlines and apparel manufacturers are among the advertisers that have applied advertising pressure on newspapers. For example, Northwest Airlines stopped advertising in the Minneapolis *Star Tribune* and St. Paul *Pioneer Press* after the papers carried stories critical of the airline's request for state funding to build maintenance bases. The advertising boycott started after the airline's vice president for communications and promotions denounced the *Star Tribune* in an opinion article for printing an advertisement critical of the airline's lobbying campaign. The airline executive felt that the newspaper should not have carried the critical ad, writing: "If the newspaper's purpose in accepting the scurrilous and slanderous attack for publication was to turn the stomachs and ruin the Thanksgiving dinners in the homes of Northwest's 18,000 Minnesota employees, you succeeded brilliantly" (Marcotty, 1992, p. 1D). The airline also banished *City Pages,* a free alternative newspaper, from its Twin Cities property after that paper carried a series of stories critical of the airline's lobbying. Since the airline didn't advertise in *City Pages*, it was unable to exert advertising pressure on it.

In an example of self-censorship, the *San Francisco Examiner* killed a column written by *Examiner* columnist Stephanie Salter in 1997, who criticized the "twisted values" of Nike, as exhibited in the "wretched excess" of the Nike Town superstore in San Francisco. Editorial-page editor Jim Finefrock chose not to run the column because it could potentially harm the newspaper's planned

Nike-sponsored "Bay to the Breakers" race (Cooper, 1997a).

Although the anecdotal evidence of advertisers pressuring newspapers to kill or alter new stories is compelling, this is also systematically-collected evidence suggesting that ad pressures on newspapers are widespread. A 1992 survey conducted among members of the Society of American Business Editors and Writers, a professional association of reporters and editors in print and broadcast, found that advertising pressures were "getting worse." Of the 55 anonymous members who completed questionnaires at the society's 1992 annual conference, more than 80 percent reported that advertiser pressure was a growing problem and 55 percent reported that advertiser pressure had compromised editorial integrity at their medium (*Atlanta Journal and Constitution*, 1992).

A questionnaire sent to 250 daily newspaper city editors, and completed by 147, reported very similar results: 55.1 percent reported that there had been "pressure from within [their] paper to write or tailor news stories to please advertisers" (Soley and Craig, 1992). To the question, "Has any advertiser succeeded in influencing news or features in your newspaper?" 36.7 percent answered "yes." To the question, "has there been pressure from within your paper to write or tailor news stories to please advertisers?" 55.1 percent reported "yes." Thus, over half of the editors reported being pressured to write or tailor stories to please advertisers.

The editors' open-ended responses pointed a finger at both the publisher and the advertising department as the internal sources of pressure. One wrote, "Yes. By the publisher." Another wrote, "Yes. Ad Department." One editor wrote, "Only internal pressure [is] from ad side. My role is to keep them away from News Department." Another wrote, "The ad department is forever submitting requests from advertisers for covering a new store, etc. When the subject is newsworthy, we run it; when we determine that it is not, we respectfully decline."

Ironically, marketing professors Rotfeld and Lasher (1994, 1994a), who concluded there is very little pressure on newspapers to appease advertisers, based their conclusions on self-reports by newspaper advertising managers and publishers, whom this survey indicated were the major sources of internal pressure.

Other questions asked by Soley and Craig (1992) concerned advertisers' attempts to influence the "news or features" appearing in the paper. To journalists, news stories are those written under a "breaking" deadline, whereas features usually are not. "Features are often interpretive, give background, play up human interest and convey the color of an event" (Hough, 1995, p. 464). The questions included:

Percent Respondents
Reporting "Yes"

Are you aware of an attempt by
any advertiser to influence what
news or features appeared in your
newspaper?   88.4

Has any advertiser tried to influence the content of a news story or feature?	89.8
Has an advertiser tried to kill a story at your newspaper?	71.4

Thus, just fewer than 90 percent reported that advertisers had attempted to influence news and features stories. Nearly 90 percent (89.8 percent) reported that advertisers attempted to influence the content of news stories. More than 70 percent of the editors reported that advertisers "tied to kill" stories at their paper. Overall, the questions indicate that advertiser pressure on newspapers is pervasive.

Two questions on the survey concerned the economic pressure that advertisers either threatened to exert or exerted on newspapers. The questions and their results are:

	Percent Respondents Reporting "Yes"
Has any advertiser threatened to withdraw advertising from your paper because of the content of stories?	93.2
Has any advertiser ever withdrawn advertising in response to the content of your newspaper?	89.1

Ninety-three percent of the editors reported that advertisers had threatened to withdraw their advertising because of the content of news stories. Almost the same percentage (i.e., 89.1 percent) reported that advertisers actually withdrew their advertising because of stories carried by the paper. Apparently, very few newspapers — only about 10 percent — have not had advertisers apply economic pressure on them.

The editors' comments about the questions are also very informative. While some advertising and marketing professors have downplayed advertiser pressures, several editors who provided open-ended responses on the questionnaires indicated advertiser pressure is common. One editor wrote: "Anyone who worked for a newspaper any length of time would know the answers to these questions." Another wrote, "Of course advertisers have tried to influence the content of stories. Most people do."

Several editors' comments suggest that a few large advertisers — such as auto dealers — may be responsible for much of the pressure. One editor wrote:

> The main offenders are our biggest advertisers, the car dealers. They all want stories involving auto sales to have a rosy outlook, and they whine about negative economic stories, even if they're on on a national level from AP [Associated Press].

Another wrote:

> The worst offenders are car dealers. One cancelled $9,000 a month in advertising after the news department

wrote a story that was not critical but
the headline writer described the car as
a "funny-looking car."

A third wrote:

A local [auto] dealer withdrew its advertising for two months after we ran a
page-one story outlining a problem with
a [model of car]. The... wire story was
accompanied by a local sidebar indi-
cating [local owners] experienced no
similar problems. The same dealer [un-
successfully] tried to convince our
city's three new car dealers to withdraw their ads.

The editors' comments also suggest that editors define
"the amount of pressure," not in terms of the number of
demands advertisers make, but by the amount they spend.
In relation to a question on whether advertisers succeed in
influencing content, one editor wrote, "Yes. But it
depends on how big the advertising account is. Small advertiser threats are generally ignored."

The biggest problem, yet the one most difficult to
study, was summarized by one editor, who wrote:

The real problem is much more subtle
and, I suspect, far more widespread...
In 13 years, at three newspapers, I have
never had a publisher who wasn't a member of the Chamber of Commerce, never
had a member who didn't at least attend
Rotary if he wasn't actually a member,
have never seen a newspaper official who

wasn't in some way tied into the local power structure.

The danger is not an overt threat. I haven't seen a publisher come back from a Chamber meeting and say, "Hey, Al at the [auto] dealer said we have to have a story about xxx." But there is a similar world view, a similar feeling about what is important and what isn't, a likeness of mind about what the newspaper should be covering. They don't need to be told by an advertiser that something is important or that a news story should focus in a particular direction. Editors and publishers probably don't think about advertisers when they make those decisions. They don't need to. They already share the same attitudes, convictions and world views.

BULLYING BROADCASTERS

There are more broadcasting stations in the United States than daily newspapers. There are 1,500 daily newspapers, but 10,500 commercial radio stations and 1,250 commercial television stations. Although there is usually just one daily newspaper in a city, there are usually many broadcasting stations, which compete for audiences and advertising dollars.

Among television stations, there is also a uniformity of programming: Nearly every station in medium and large cities produces Sunday morning talk shows and weekday evening newscasts, and carries a mix of syndicated and network programs consisting of situation comedies, serials, dramas, news and entertainment "magazines." As a consequence, companies should find television advertising on one station substitutable for advertising on another. Advertisers can move from one station to another in search of lower advertising rates, or can move from one to another if angered by programming content.

A similar situation exists with radio. While there are numerous formats, such as talk, sports, news, oldies, easy listening and classic rock, there are frequently several radio stations in a city with similar programming. Even if the formats of radio stations are different, the stations can still deliver the same demographic group to an advertiser, making competition among radio stations for advertising dollars quite fierce. For example, the sports and progressive rock formats tend to deliver the same, demographic group — younger males — which gives advertisers seeking to target this group a wide array of choices. Given the competitive nature of the radio medium, it should be far more susceptible to advertising pressure than either newspapers or television: Advertisers can easily switch their advertising from one station to another if angered by the content of programming.

The anecdotal evidence suggests that advertisers are aware of the competition among television stations and networks for advertising revenues, and use this competition to influence news reports. The evidence suggests that advertisers are even willing to pressure large, influential electronic media, such as the USA cable and ABC television networks. For example, Johnson & Johnson, the nation's fifth largest advertiser, reportedly pressured the USA network into cancelling, "Who Killed Sue Snow?," a movie about murders committed with cyanide-laced Tylenol in 1982. Johnson & Johnson, the manufacturer of Tylenol, feared the program would bring back memories of the scare or trigger copycat attacks. Although Johnson & Johnson denies explicitly threatening the network with ad cancellations, it admits having discussed its concerns with network executives, who later cancelled the show (Sepinwall, 2000).

When a segment of ABC's "20/20" news magazine examined some of the pitfalls of buying a car from dealers, auto dealers pulled their advertising from several ABC affiliates (*Broadcasting,* 1989). This type of pressure has had enduring effects. In Chicago, ABC-owned station WLS-TV killed an "Inside Edition" story several years later about fire hazards in Ford vehicles because it "didn't want to risk offending auto dealers who advertise heavily on the station." The episode was scheduled the week that the station was sponsoring Chicago's biggest auto show (Kurtz, 1996).

In 1995, when a segment of ABC's "Primetime Live" carried a story about the hidden costs of car leasing that bent-over-backward to be balanced, the affiliate in Buffalo, New York decided against carrying the program, and WXYZ-TV, the ABC-affiliate in Detroit, carried a follow-up discussion about leasing during its news programs in an effort to appease automobile advertisers (Pergament, 1996).

Detroit's WXYZ-TV has had other problems with automobile dealers. In 1999, reporter Shellee Smith did a story on auto dealer Mel Farr, a former Detroit Lions football player, whose dealership was accused of charging illegally high interest rates and of repossessing cars from buyers when Farr failed to find financing for them. Farr refused to grant Smith an interview about the accusations, but news director Dave Roberts convinced him to tell his side of the story to anchor Guy Gordon, which he did. Farr refused to respond directly to Gordon's questions about the allegations. Instead, the football player-turned-auto dealer stated that it "seems to me the bigger story should be that Mel Farr, an African American, ex-Detroit Lions football player, took a bankrupt dealership [to] $596 million in sales in 1999." After the interview, Farr cancelled his six-figure advertising contract with the station (Trigoboff, 1999).

Some stations have gone even further than killing stories and sacking reporters to appease advertisers. Cincinnati station WLWT-TV reportedly allowed auto dealers to prescreen a story by consumer affairs reporter Noel Morgan about rental cars being sold as factory official cars, and then allowed the dealers to prepare a response to the story. The dealers were allowed to practice "their responses on cue cards," reported Morgan, whose contract with the station was not renewed (Collins, 1992, pp. 22-23).

Stories about automobile dealers pressuring television news rooms are not the only stories about advertiser pressures to surface. Other large advertisers, such as airlines, department stores and drug stores, have also pressured news rooms into killing stores about their sales practices (Beck, 1990; Weisbaum, 1990). Stations in large cities, as well as small cities, have been pressured. For example,

WHDH-TV of Boston axed a story critical of American Airlines, apparently because of advertiser pressure. When asked about killing the story, WHDH-TV general manager Mike Carson defended the decision, saying that he was "proud decisions were made by our news management to not release a story before we have all of the details and evaluate its impact on the entire industry" (Biddle, 1995).

To determine whether the stories about advertiser pressures are the exception or the rule, a questionnaire about advertiser pressures was sent to one reporter at every commercial television station employing a member of Investigative Reporters and Editors (IRE), an organization of news reporters.[1] The questionnaires asked reporters about advertiser muscling of their news operations, their stations' responses to these pressures, and the sizes of their cities. Only one IRE member at each station was sent a questionnaire, thereby eliminating duplicated answers. Just under 50 percent (i.e., 49.8 percent) of the questionnaires sent out were completed and returned. Unlike the survey of newspaper editors, this one restricted answers to "the last three years" and included "don't know" as possible responses.

Nearly three-quarters of the reporters and editors (i.e., 74.2 percent) reported that advertisers had "tried to influence the content" of news at their stations. The majority of respondents -- 60 percent -- also reported that advertisers had attempted to kill stories.

Moreover, the responses show that advertisers use monetary leverage as part of their pressure. More than two-thirds (i.e., 68.3 percent) reported that advertisers threatened to withdraw their advertising because of the content of news stories. Forty-four percent of the respondents reported that advertisers had "actually withdrawn advertising because of the content of a news report."

The responses of reporters at large and small market stations did not differ. For example, 75 percent of respondents at large market stations reported that advertisers had "tried to influence the content" of news stories, compared to 74 percent of respondents at small market stations. As for whether advertisers had actually "withdrawn advertising because of the content of a news report," 44.2 percent of reporters at stations in both large and small markets responded affirmatively.

Comments made on the questionnaires suggest that automobile dealers are a major source of censorial pressure. One respondent wrote, "It would be interesting for you to take a look at the role car dealers play in governing what's said about them by local television. They are practically untouchable."

Citing another censorious industry, one reporter noted that "we are currently battling with the local restaurant association and the members who advertise on our station whether we should air the city's weekly restaurant inspection ratings." The reporter added, "In this instance, my bosses are backing me." Grocery stores and "lawyers who advertise on television" were also mentioned as sources of pressure.

Of course, the more important question is not whether advertisers have directly pressured television stations, but whether the stations have yielded to the pressure. Questioned whether advertisers "succeeded in influencing a news report at your station," nearly as many said their stations had capitulated (40 percent) as had withstood the pressure (43 percent). Seventeen percent reported that they "don't know" whether their stations capitulated.

Two questions addressed the issue of self-censorship. Asked whether there had been "pressure from within your stations to not produce news stories that advertisers might find objectionable," 59 percent of respondents said there had been. One respondent wrote, "I have experienced direct pressure from my general manager (with no defense from my news director) to not only tread lightly on advertisers, but also to be careful about our corporate neighbors in the community. Disgusting!"

A reporter in California, who claimed to have been sacked for offending advertisers, sent a copy of a memo he received from his news director, reading, "If you're involved in a story which you know might reflect badly on an advertiser, please let me know, so I can give sales a heads up."

Several respondents provided in-depth descriptions of the internal pressures at their stations. One wrote, "I've found that many general managers at TV stations (including my own) are former TV sales people and therefore know the advertisers very well. It is common for advertisers to call a station and express their concerns about a story. While I have never been asked to lie or mislead viewers, I have been asked to soften a story an advertiser might find objectionable."

Another commented that "I'm not sure if pressure is the right word. It is probably better described as story steering. For example, if a story is suggested on car dealers, something might be said like, there's a lot better things for us to look into, don't you think?" Similarly, one reporter wrote that direct pressure wasn't applied at the station, but there was "just a general understanding to avoid a specific area."

As for whether there had "been pressure from within your station to produce news stories to please advertisers," 56 percent of respondents reported that there was. Several reporters wrote comments about this pressure. The most frequent comment suggested that "sales people come in and request stories be done on their clients" or that sales people set up "interviews and tell us about them after they're promised." Another wrote there was pressure "to interview advertisers on positive stories and not on negative stories with the guidance of management."

Other reporters painted a less benevolent picture of the pressure to produce stories to please advertisers. One wrote that the "pressure to produce stories to please advertisers is commonplace and intense. As an example, a reporter is doing an annual Valentines Day Gifts feature. Management will strongly suggest visiting a florist that advertises with the station." The reporter also described an incident where the news director told a business reporter to do a story on an advertiser, saying, "We have to do a story on this. I know it isn't news, but this is a huge account. The reporter knew she had no choice and did the story. . . .These types of incidents happen on a weekly, if not daily, basis to varying degrees."

Another reporter provided a directive that had been handed down by the news director: "From time to time, we do stories where we need an expert of sorts . . . no one company or person in particular, just someone who knows about a certain subject. Sales has asked me to check with them in those situations, feeling that . . . we might as well call on one who does business with the station. So, whenever it's one of those situations (like we need a realtor, we need a bail bondsman, we need a coffee shop owner), please give sales a call and see if they have someone who's available and media friendly." As for the sources of internal pressure, 35 reporters specifically mentioned the sales manager or sales department as being the source of pressure, 23 mentioned the general manager or "management," and nine mentioned the news director.

While other groups try to influence or suppress coverage, advertisers wield a unique economic club over television stations by withdrawing or threatening to withdraw advertising. However, advertisers do not exert the pressure by themselves. As one respondent wrote:

> The pressure comes from outside the
> station and within the station and often
> the two sides are working together to
> either kill stories or alter them. I know
> of an instance where a sales executive
> actually met with the focus of an in-
> vestigative report over lunch and told
> him what the story would be about. How
> did the sales executive know the content
> of an investigative report before it aired?
> A news executive told him.

Not all news executives have sold out, of course. But with pressures for greater profits, the incentive to provide news stories that will either please or not offend advertisers is great. The problem was summarized by an investigative reporter, who wrote:

> The pressure from outside influences
> doesn't bother me; it's always been there
> and I suspect it always will be. However,
> there seems to be a frightening trend
> for the powers that be at corporate [head-
> quarters] to give in to that pressure and
> pretend everything will go on as before,
> business as usual.

Another survey conducted by the Pew Research Center (1999) suggests that ad pressures, while a problem, are not as endemic as these responses suggest. The Pew survey asked working journalists and media executives, "In your opinion, to what extent do advertising concerns influence news organizations' decisions about which stories to cover or emphasize?" One-quarter of journalists at national media, including the broadcast networks, prestigious newspapers, magazines, and one-third of journalists at local media reported that advertising concerns had a "great deal" or "fair amount" of influence on news reporting at their medium. Although the results suggest that advertising pressure is not as pervasive as the other survey results suggest, they do show that advertisers are influencing media content -- even at the largest media.

MUSCLING MAGAZINES

Although magazines are usually described as a single medium, advertisers and publishers classify magazines by their audiences, circulation type, and purpose. There are farm, consumer, and business magazines, which are distributed differently. Farm publications are a distinctive class of magazines because farming is both a lifestyle and a business. Farm publications, such as *Southeastern Peanut Farmer* and *North Dakota Stockman*, are often distributed regionally. Most are "controlled circulation," meaning that they are sent for free to specific farmers. Consumer magazines are sold by subscriptions or single copies, which are available through retailers and news stands. These publications are available to the general public. Business or trade publications are sometimes sold, but are most often distributed through the mail for free to employees within an industry or to members of professional associations.

There is substantial evidence that advertisers influence the content of all three classes of magazines, but that the influence differs by the class of magazine. Advertisers have much more influence over the content of farm magazines than either consumer or business magazines, according to a study conducted by University of Illinois professors Robert Hays and Ann Reisner (1990), who surveyed farm magazine writers. Their survey found that 47 percent of writers believed that farm magazines' efforts to please advertisers made it difficult to work "at arm's length, without any kind of vested interest." Over one-third of farm writers (37 percent) reported that advertisers' attempts to influence editorial material was harming agricultural journalism, while an additional 50 percent reported that the practice was a "problem in some cases."

Thirty-seven percent of the farm writers reported pressure from advertisers or editors to slant stories to please advertisers was harming the profession. An additional 32 percent reported that this was an occasional problem. Based on these responses, professors Hays and Reisner (1990) concluded that "advertiser-related pressure on farm magazine writers and editors is a serious problem." The problem exits because farm magazines "have a somewhat narrow advertising base. The inherent danger of losing a single advertiser that might be displeased by unfavorable editorial content necessarily weighs more heavily on the minds of farm magazine editors and publishers" than editors and publishers of consumer or business magazines (Hays and Reisner, 1990, p. 941).

A survey of consumer and business magazine editors conducted by *Folio* magazine, a trade publication for magazine managers, found that 41.2 percent of consumer magazine editors and 40.2 percent of business publication editor had "been told by the ad director or the publisher to do something that seriously compromised editorial" integrity. Of the business publications editors who were pressured, 40 percent said they protest but do what the ad director or publisher requested. Fewer than half said that they would "just say no" to the request (Howland, 1989).

Consumer magazine editors were much more likely to turn down requests to please advertisers. Almost three-quarters of the consumer magazine editors reported that they would rebuff pressures to compromise editorial integrity. However, 66.1 percent of editors said it was "appropriate for an ad director to ask an editor to have lunch with an advertiser" and 67.7 percent reported that it was "acceptable for an ad director to personally deliver a press release from the advertiser to the director." This is a far different situation than existed in past times, according to Elizabeth Crowe, the president and editorial director of Gruner + Jahr, USA, a magazine publisher. Crowe says that when she started in the industry in the 1960s, it "was thought that any contact between advertising and editorial would result in hopeless corruption" (Howland, 1989, p. 95).

In the past few years, consumer magazines have been compromised even more, as the industry has been forced to compete with the internet for advertising dollars. Even the largest, most prestigious publications have knuckled under to advertising pressures. According to G. Bruce Knecht (1997) of the *Wall Street Journal*, many large advertisers, including Chrysler Corp., Ford Motor Co., Ameritech and Bell South, now demand that magazine publishers provide them with prior notice when an issue in which they are advertising contains "controversial" stories or opinion.

To assure that publishers comply with advertisers' demands concerning story content, the companies' advertising agencies send notices to publishers telling them about their rules concerning content. If a magazine violates the rules, the advertising gets yanked. This can be costly to a magazine like *Esquire*, which gets about $56,500 for a one-page, four-color advertisement (Standard Rate & Data Service , 1999, p. 587).

A letter sent to publishers by PentaCom, Chrysler's advertising agency, stated, "In an effort to avoid potential conflicts, it is required that Chrysler Corporation be alerted in advance of any and all editorial content that encompasses sexual, political, social issues or any editorial that might be construed as provocative or offensive." The Young & Rubicam advertising agency also admitted that it has warned publishers about producing stories it "considers antisocial or in bad taste," while an Ameritech spokesperson said the company steered clear of "anything controversial" (Knecht, 1997).

Advertisers were not bluffing about pulling their advertising. *Sports Illustrated* lost more than $1 million in golf ads after doing a story on lesbian golf fans at the Dinah Shore tournament in Palm Springs. IBM and its software subsidiary Lotus withdrew its advertising from *Fortune* after the magazine carried a less-than-flattering profile of IBM's chief executive, Louis Gerstner, Jr. (Pogrebin, 1997). Ford pulled six months' worth of car ads from the *New Yorker* after a full-page pitch for Mercury ran next to a story that quoted Nine Inch Nails' explicit rock lyrics. After Ford's action, the *New Yorker* compiled a list of about 50 sensitive advertisers who are given "heads ups" if the magazine plans to carry controversial or potentially offensive materials (Shaw, 1998).

Some publishers have apparently become very cautious about what they print as a result of the letters and ad cancellations. *Esquire* cancelled a story containing a few explicit words about a gay man who writes college term papers in exchange for sex. The story was killed out of fear that it would violate Chrysler's rules about controversial content (Shaw, 1998).

In response to widespread publicity about Chrysler's advertising policies, and assertions that it amounted to censorship, the corporation announced that it would no longer prescreen magazines because magazine editors know "what our advertising guidelines are. There is no need for prenotification anymore." At the time this announcement, a Chrysler spokesperson said, "We've become the poster child for alleged censorship, when in fact we feel our policy is one of the easiest guidelines... to work with." Despite the announced change in policy, the corporation hinted that it would nonetheless withdraw its advertising from magazines with controversial content. The spokesperson said that the company is "less likely to take a chance on publications with an editorial edge in the future" (Phillips, 1997).

Advertisers with staid, conservative images are not the only ones that muscle magazines. In 1998, Coca-Cola's advertising agency sent a letter to publishers outlining their requirements for compatible editorial material. Publishers who place Coca-cola advertisements near "inappropriate editorial matter will be subject to a full makegood," the letter warned. The letter stated that Coke ads were to be near "positive and upbeat" editorial material, not near "Hard news; Sex related issues; Drugs (Prescription or Illegal); Medicine (e.g., chronic illnesses such as cancer, diabetes, AIDS, etc.); Health (e.g., mental or physical medical conditions); Negative diet information (e.g., bulimia, anorexia, quick weight loss, etc.); Food; Political issues; Articles containing vulgar language; Religion" (Ledbetter, 1998). The list leaves out nearly everything but celebrity fluff and movie and recording reviews.

Advertisers are not the only businesses that pressure magazine publishers about content. Retail chains are also a source of pressure and wield considerable influence because they control large percentages of consumer magazine single-copy sales. Supermarkets and discount stores control 55 percent of single-copy sales; Wal-Mart alone controls nine percent.

The Winn-Dixie supermarket chain with 1,186 stores, Walgreen's drug store chain with 2,363 stores, and the Kroger supermarket chain with 1,300 stores are among the other retailers, in addition to Wal-Mart, that prescreen magazines or request that publishers provide them with an advance warning that controversial material will be carried in the magazine. The retailers then decide whether they will sell the magazine.

The retailers report that they screen magazines to a-void getting complaints from customers, but the retailers do not have clear policies about what is and isn't acceptable. As Walgreen's spokesperson Michael Polzin said, "We don't have written guidelines that we send to distributors, but they know what we're concerned about" (Knecht, 1997a, p. A13). Winn-Dixie refused to carry an issue of *Cosmopolitan*, the largest selling magazine in single-copy sales, when a cover headline read, "His & Her Orgasms," and Wal-Mart refused to carry an issue of *Vibe*, an urban culture magazine, because of a risque photo of singer Toni Braxton on the cover. While most of the retail censorship concerns sexual material, the absence of clear policies allows retailers to refuse magazines with "articles on controversial subjects such as abortion, homosexuality and religion" (Knecht, 1997a, p. A13).

Magazines are not alone in having their content censored or shaped by retailers. Manufacturers of compact disks and motion picture videotapes have also been pressured to change content or be banished from the shelves of Wal-Mart, Kmart, Blockbuster and other large retailers. Wal-Mart, which sells nearly 10 percent of the compact disks in the United States, has refused to carry recordings that carry "parental advisory" stickers. The Arkansas-based retailer demands that recording companies produce tamer versions of their recordings to stock in Wal-Mart stores, with controversial or objectionable lyrics edited out, and risque portions of photos airbrushed out. Record companies and recording artists usually acquiesce to Wal-Mart's request for a different version of a recording because of the retailer's huge sales. Even superstars like John Mellencamp acquiesce to these demands, even if the demand doesn't concern sexual or violent content. Wal-Mart requested that images of Jesus and the devil be airbrushed off the cover of the Mellencamp album, "Mr. Happy Go-Lucky," and Mellencamp complied (*San Francisco Chronicle*, 1996).

One artist who wouldn't comply was Sheryl Crow, whose song "Love Is a Good Thing" contained the lyrics, "Watch our children while they kill each other with a gun they bought at the Wal-Mart discount stores." Wal-Mart demanded that Crow delete the lyrics, or be banished from their stores. The chain claimed that the lyrics were irresponsible and unfair, even though Wal-Mart has been sued twice by relatives of victims killed by Wal-Mart -

purchased guns. Crow refused. The ban cost Crow an estimated half a million in sales (Schoemer, 1996; Stewart, 1996).

TROUBLE BREWING

Advertiser pressures and media self-censorship are serious issues, not just because they deprive citizens of information, but because they place impediments in the way of others' speech. Citizens groups that advocate policies opposed by large advertisers are not just banished from news stories, they even find it difficult to buy advertising time to disseminate their views. Major media are not willing to sell advertising time or space to advocacy groups that might offend large advertisers with their messages. As a consequence, these opposition views are rarely heard.

Under current law, the commercial media determine the advertisers to which they are willing to sell time or space *(Columbia Broadcasting System, Inc. v. Democratic National Committee, Inc*, 1972; *Chicago Joint Board v. Chicago Tribune Co*., 1970). A television station or newspaper can refuse to sell advertising for any reason -- not just because the ad is offensive, although "offensiveness" and "distastefulness" are frequently used excuses for refusing to carry issue ads. When a peace group, Neighbor to Neighbor, tried to buy television commercials in 1990 calling for a boycott of Folgers coffee, a brand marketed by Procter & Gamble, the country's largest advertiser, Boston stations WBZ-TV and WCVB-TV refused to sell it time. The commercial, which suggested that money from coffee sales helped prolong the Salvadorean civil war, ended with blood dripping from a coffee cup. Anthony Vinciquerra, the general sales manager of WBZ-TV, called the commercial "terribly distasteful," adding that the claims made in the commercial lacked substantiation. WCVB-TV public relations director Burt Peretsky said his station didn't normally accept issue advertising except during elections, but had also rejected the commercial because it called "for damage to a particular product" (Palmer, 1990).

Although WBZ-TV and WCVB-TV rejected the commercial, WHDH-TV aired it twice, causing Procter & Gamble to cancel $1 million in advertising on the station. Procter & Gamble cancelled its advertising for all brands — Pampers, Tide, Crest, Oil of Olay and Charmin -- not just Folgers. When cancelling the ads, Procter & Gamble warned that it would cancel advertising on any station that aired the "distasteful" commercial (Stencel, 1990). Stations apparently heeded Procter & Gamble's warning. Boston television stations also refused to sell Neighbor to Neighbor advertising for a 1993 advertising campaign that called for a "single payer" national health plan, similar to the one in Canada. Using a General Accounting Office report as its source, the commercial stated that "if we get rid of health insurance companies, we can have complete coverage for everyone for the same money."

Although the commercial was not offensive, it was nevertheless rejected by WHDH-TV and three other Boston television stations. Fearful that it would lose health insurance industry advertising, as it had Procter & Gamble advertising, WHDH-TV announced that it would not air the commercial because "the issue is not addressed in a comprehensive manner in a 30-second format and [the station] will address it itself in a longer form sometime in the future" (*United Press International*, 1993).

Boston isn't the only market where advocates of a single payer national health plan have had difficulty buying time. Washington, DC stations refused to sell commercials to an advocacy group, the Campaign for Health Security, which asked, "Why don't we get rid of health insurance companies?" WRC-TV, owned and operated by NBC, said in rejecting the commercials that statements in the ad weren't supported by facts. "Statements which are presented as facts have to be substantiated," a station spokesperson explained, even though the station had been given an article from the prestigious *New England Journal of Medicine* that reached the same conclusion as the commercials, and the *New England Journal* findings were publicized by a page three story in the *Washington Post* a few weeks earlier (Shone, 1993).[2]

While refusing to sell commercial time to the consumer group, the stations ran numerous commercials unsupported by facts for health insurance companies and the Health Insurance Associations of America, which backed a mixture of public and private insurance (Shone, 1993).

Washington, DC stations also refused to sell commercial time to another consumer group, the Health Care Reform Project, whose commercials criticized Pizza Hut for not providing health insurance for newly-hired workers. Pizza Hut, a large television advertiser, warned the stations in a letter not to run the commercials, and not one did. One station said that it wasn't influenced by the letter; it rejected the commercial because the appeal was "purely emotional" (Kurtz, 1994).

In the Twin Cities, television stations refused to sell commercial time to the Prairie Island Sioux community, which produced a commercial critical of Northern States Power Company's plan to store spent nuclear fuel rods on the island. When rejecting the Sioux community's request to buy advertising time, the television stations claimed that the commercials, which were professionally produced by an advertising agency, didn't meet their standards of professionalism. Northern States Power, the local utility monopoly, was a large advertiser on the television stations (Grow, 1991).

In Detroit, radio stations refused to sell advertising time to the United Auto Workers, which was calling for a boycott of Hudson department stores following the corporation's intimidation of union organizers. Hudson was a large advertiser on the stations (*Minneapolis Star Tribune*, 1991).

During the 1997 test marketing in Cedar Rapids and Waterloo, Iowa of Frito-Lay potato chips made with Olestra, KCRG-TV and KWWL-TV refused to sell commercial time to the Center for Science in the Public Interest. The Center's television commercials described some of the health problems posed by Olestra. In New Jersey, the *Asbury Park Press* refused to run an advertisement produced by local community groups that criticized several beer companies' "marketing beer to children" during the Halloween holiday season. The newspaper said it would run the ad if the names of the beer companies were removed (Cooper, 1997b).

"Offensive" was the excuse given by billboard companies, which refused to sell space for a 1999 anti-meat campaign sponsored by People for the Ethical Treatment of Animals (PETA). Billboard advertising is used extensively by the dairy and beef industries to promote consumption. The U.S. Dairy Producers, the 72nd largest advertiser in the country, relies extensively on billboards, as does McDonald's, the largest seller of beef in the world. McDonald's was the 14th largest advertiser in the United States in 1998 (*Advertising* Age, 1999).

The banished PETA billboard showed a bikini-clad model holding a string of sausages with the headline, "I Threw a Party But the Cattlemen Couldn't Come." Underneath was the line, "Eating Meat Can Cause Impotence." The purpose of the billboard was to promote vegetarianism by linking meat-eating and impotence, for which there is some medical evidence. The evidence suggests that arteriosclerosis, which restricts blood flow, is higher for individuals who have high levels of saturated fats in their diets, and restricted blood flow can lead to impotence. Meat and dairy products are major sources of saturated fats.

Billboard companies in Wisconsin, Minnesota, Texas, Kansas, Nebraska, Oklahoma and Colorado refused PETA's campaign, citing "offensiveness" as the reason. Michael Aloia, general manager of Chancellor Outdoor Advertising, which rejected the campaign for its billboards in Wisconsin and Minnesota, said, "What we like to do with any political advertising is, we prefer to have positive messages about the cause. We also have policies with regard to sexual orientation or sexual connotations," which the PETA campaign failed to meet (Rosenberg, 1999).

Even messages that are unoffensive, unemotional and do not target a specific product have been rejected by the mass media. The Media Foundation, which publishes *Adbusters* magazine and opposes the over-commercialization of society, has had difficulty finding media that will accept advertisements for its annual "Buy Nothing Day." These "un-commercials" urge people to boycott businesses one day a year to protest crass consumerism. *Adbusters* editor Kalle Lasn reports that the un-commercials are routinely rejected by station managers with comments such as, "Well, why should we shoot ourselves in the foot by running your ads. We don't have to work against our legitimate business interests" (Seaman, 1997).

Although the media refuse to sell community and activist groups advertising time to criticize large advertisers, this form of censorship occurs far less frequently than news censorship. The reason is that community and activist groups can rarely scrape together the money to buy advertising time. Activist groups like Neighbor to Neighbor survive on donations from individuals; corporations rarely donate to such groups.

Instead, corporations fund groups such as the Coalition for Health Insurance Choices, a front for the Health Insurance Associations of America; the National Smokers Alliance, an organization created and funded by the tobacco industry; the Partnership for a Competitive Texas, a front for AT&T; and Wisconsin Manufacturing and Commerce, an ostensibly nonpartisan organization that spent hundreds of thousands of dollars on issue ads attacking Democrats and liberals. These business front groups, sometimes refereed to "astroturf organizations" because they lack real grassroots, are well-funded and buy huge amounts of advertising. Their advertisements are never rejected by the media, even when emotional, unfair and clearly deceptive.

The Coalition for Health Insurance Choices (CHIC) ran a multimillion dollar advertising campaign featuring fictitious characters named "Harry" and "Louise" that opposed former President Clinton's health care proposals. Although the group was not a coalition as claimed -- it had no membership or funding except from the health insurance company trade association, the Health Insurance Associations of America -- it had no difficulty buying advertising time on radio and television stations, including some that refused to carry commercials favoring a "single payer" plan. The CHIC campaign became the focus of many media stories, and the trade group "considered the bulk of this coverage to be very positive" (Bodensteiner, 1997; Foisie, 1994).

In California, the National Smokers Alliance ran a newspaper advertising campaign against California's smoking restrictions, claiming that they hurt business and were "discriminatory." The Alliance, which existed only on paper, was the creation of the Philip Morris tobacco company and was industry-funded (Hayward, 1995). In Texas, a television advertising campaign was waged by the Partnership for a Competitive Texas that featured a fictitious character, "Carolyn," who claimed that Southwestern "Bell and GTE are fighting so hard to stop competition." The campaign suggested that the Partnership was a grass roots group that advocated telecommunication deregulation. In reality, the Partnership and the advertising campaign were created and funded by AT&T, a Bell and GTE competitor (Barker, 1999).

In Wisconsin, Wisconsin Manufacturers & Commerce, a business-funded group that refuses to reveal the sources of its funding, and Americans for Job Security, an Washington, DC-based organization funded by insurance and paper companies, purchased numerous "issue ads" supporting Republican candidates and attacking Democrats in the 1998 elections, despite a state ban on business involvement in elections and a state law requiring the disclosure of campaign contributors. The groups claimed that they were running issue ads, not campaign ads, because the commercials did not explicitly recommend voting for Republican candidates. Television stations accepted these groups' deceptions and a half-million dollars from their advertising.

Business front groups such as these exist for nearly every industry and in every state, giving corporations an incomparably large voice in policy debates. The seeming ease with which "astroturf" groups buy advertising time and the difficulties consumer groups have suggests that commercial media have two standards for accepting ads: One standard is for well-heeled advertisers like Calvin Klein and the Coalition for Health Insurance Choices, which are free to create offensive, emotional or deceptive ads. The other is for community and activist organizations, whose advertisements are rejected whenever they jeopardize an advertising account, even when the assertions can be documented. For example, WHDH-TV hired former *Washington Post* reporter Scott Armstrong to investigate claims in Neighbor to Neighbor's anti-Folgers commercial after Procter & Gamble initiated its boycott. When the investigation was complete, WHDH-TV refuse to publicly release Armstrong's report, claiming that it was confidential. However, parts of the report were leaked to activist groups. The leaked portions reported that Salvadorean coffee producers "have been tied, historically and up to the present, to human rights violations against coffee workers, union leaders and other peasants." The report concluded that Salvadorean death squads have received "continuous financing from the coffee industry since the late 1970s" (Higgins, 1991).

Although the report remained confidential, Procter & Gamble criticized its findings, claiming that it was filled with "false and misleading information." The corporation dismissed the findings, saying there was "no evidence from any reliable source linking our coffee purchases to violence in El Salvador" (Higgins, 1991).

Similarly, stations rejected commercials supporting a single payer health plan even though there was documentation supporting the advertisements' conclusions. Facts are apparently irrelevant when they go against the interest of large advertisers.

COUNTERING ADVERTISING CENSORSHIP

In the United States, the only social entity with the finances and power to stand up to corporate giants like Procter & Gamble and automobile manufacturers is the federal government. Unfortunately, the government has taken a laissez faire attitude toward corporate activities – mergers, takeovers, and monopolistic selling practices – since the early 1980s.

For nearly two decades, U.S. citizens have been bombarded by a nearly endless campaign, much of it funded by corporations, asserting that the federal government is too big, too powerful, and too unresponsive to citizens. The result has been a steady stream of deregulation that has allowed corporations to increase their size, power and profit at public expense. Today, corporate power and actions are virtually unchallenged.

Government agencies such as the FCC and the FTC could easily curb advertising censorship and other undesirable business practices. Unfortunately, these agencies have also adopted laissez faire, deregulatory policies that have allowed corporate abuses to flourish. For example, the FCC rescinded the Fairness Doctrine as part of its policy of deregulation. The Fairness Doctrine required broadcasting stations to provide the public with "a reasonable opportunity to hear different opposing positions on public issues of interest and importance to the community" (Federal Communications Commission, 1949; Kahn, 1973).

During the era when it was in effect, the Fairness Doctrine was even extended to advertisements for controversial products by *Banzhaf v. FCC* (1968). As a result, the FCC ordered television and radio stations to provide response time to opponents of cigarette smoking to counter cigarette commercials, which were then allowed on broadcasting stations. After adopting this policy, the FCC soon retreated, allowing advertisements for other controversial products to go unchallenged.

If the FCC had not abrogated its responsibilities to the public by retreating on *Banzhaf* and later revoking the Fairness Doctrine, citizens would have greater access to the broadcasting airwaves, which rightfully belong to them. Broadcasting stations would be required to provide reply time to consumers who advocate a single-payer health plan, advocate boycotting harmful products or who wish to "unmask" large corporations hiding behind fictitious names, such as the Partnership for a Competitive Texas.[3]

Although broadcasting corporations have repeatedly opposed providing citizens groups with free or paid access to their stations, broadcasters do not own or even rent the frequencies on which they operate. These frequencies are legally public property, which broadcasters are allowed to use provided they serve the "public interest, convenience and necessity." The rule of that land is that broadcasters who do not serve the "public interest" are not to receive broadcasting licenses. Unfortunately, "public interest" has become synonymous with broadcasting corporations' profits in the minds of the FCC and the public, which doesn't realize that it owns the airwaves... and has a right to take them back.

Because the airwaves are public property, the FCC could adopt policies regulating broadcast advertising. It currently has regulations governing lotteries and gambling, and commercials directed to children. The FCC could also adopt policies that address advertising censorship. For example, the FCC could prohibit a broadcast station from killing a news story to please advertisers. It could require that broadcast advertising contracts contain provisions prohibiting advertisers from withdrawing their advertising to protest reportage. Although broadcasters and advertisers would whine that such regulations infringe on their First Amendment rights, the reality is quite different: The regulations would enhance the rights of the public, who have a right to expect that their airwaves deliver uncensored programming.

The same can be said for the FTC. The FTC took a small step in the right direction when it filed the restraint of trade action against the Santa Clara County Motor Dealers Association for its group boycott of the San Jose *Mercury News*. But the FTC could do more. It could adopt regulations prohibiting group boycotts by all trade associations. It could take action against groups of advertisers such as the Velva Association of Commerce that launch boycotts of their local newspapers. It could also investigate the actions of large advertising agencies such as PentaCom and Young & Rubicam that represent multiple advertisers. If an advertising agency pressures the media or threatens to withdraw advertising for more than one client, that should be declared an illegal, collusive act.

Government actions such as these are necessary if advertising censorship is to be curbed.

ENDNOTES

1. The questionnaires were sent to 241 editors and reporters on the IRE membership list with a self-addressed stamped envelope and cover letter, which assured respondents anonymity. Five days later, a follow-up postcard was sent to all 241 reporters and editors, asking them to complete and return the questionnaire, if they had not done so already.

2. See Spencer, Rich (1993, August 6). Hospital administration costs put at 25 %. *Washington Post*, p. A3. *The New England Journal of Medicine* article, written by three Harvard Medical School professors, concluded that 25 percent of U.S. hospital expenses could be saved with a Canada-style, single-payer health plan.

3. Under *Columbia Broadcasting Corporation, Inc. v. Democratic National Committee* (1972), broadcasters are not required to sell advertising to advocacy groups. However, under the Fairness Doctrine, in effect when this decision was reached, broadcasting stations would be required to sell time to groups such as the Campaign for Health Security if they sold time to business front groups such as the Coalition for Health Insurance Choices.

4. Congress did this with the FCC's proposal to license low-power FM stations.

5. Corporations have a multiplicity of means at their disposal to silence critics, including the media. Corporations can file frivolous civil suits (commonly called strategic lawsuits against public participation or SLAPPs) against the media, as Food Lion did with ABC in 1992; file product disparagement law suits, as the Texas beef industry did against Oprah Winfrey; or banish reporters and media from their property, as Northwest Airlines did to *City Pages* in 1992.

REFERENCES

Advertising Age (1999, September 27). Leading national advertisers, 1.

Associated Press (1999, April 20). Dealers spent $5.3 billion on ads. *Buffalo News,* 6E.

Associated Press (1999a, September 16). Big business reroutes PAC money. *Chicago Tribune,* 11.

Atlanta Journal and Constitution (1992, May 1). Ad pressures up, business journalists say, 2D.

Bagdikian, Ben H. (1995). *Media Monopoly.* Boston: Beacon Press.

Banks, Louis (1978, April). Memo to the press: They hate you out there. *The Atlantic,* 38.

Banzhaf v. FCC (1968) 405 F.2nd 1082. Certiorari denied (1969) 396 U.S. 842.

Barker, Max (1999, April 25). Corporations sow seeds of many grass-roots efforts. *Fort Worth Star-Telegram,* 1.

Beck, Andre (1990, Fall). A bigger chill -- The terrifying trend to clamp down on advertiser-sensitive reporting in television. *IRE Journal,* 17.

Biddle, Frederic, (1995, December 1). WHDH defends axing story. *Boston Globe,* 62.

Bodensteiner, Carol (1997, March 22). Special interest group coalitions. *Public Relations Review,* 34.

Broadcasting (1989, December 18). Some ABC affiliates feel brunt of '20/20' piece, 50.

Buckley v. Valeo (1976). 424 U.S. 1

Chicago Joint Board v. Chicago Tribune Co. (1970). 435 F. 2nd 470.

Chiuy, Yvonne (1995, August 2). FTC settles ad boycott case. *Washington Post,* F3.

Collins, Ronald K. L. (1992). *Dictating Content.* Washington, D.C.: Center for the Study of Commercialism.

Columbia Broadcasting System, Inc. v. Democratic National Committee, Inc. (1972). 412 U.S. 94.

Cooper, Gloria (1993, May). Darts and laurels. *Columbia Journalism Review,* 23.

Cooper, Gloria (1997, March/April). Darts and laurels. *Columbia Journalism Review,* 22.

Cooper, Gloria (1997a, July/August). Darts and laurels. *Columbia Journalism Review,* 21.

Cooper, Gloria (1997b, May/June,). Darts & laurels. *Columbia Journalism Review,* 23-24.

Cooper, Gloria (1998, March/April). Darts and laurels. *Columbia Journalism Review,* 15.

Cooper, Gloria (1999, January/February). Darts and laurels. *Columbia Journalism Review,* 25.

Denton, Frank (1993, September). Letter to the editor. *Columbia Journalism Review,* 8.

Donovan, Lauren (1999, March 15). Businesses pull out of Velva newspaper. *Bismarck Tribune,* 1A.

Eilperin, Juliet (1999, October 18). House whip wields fund-raising clout. *Washington Post,* A1.

Federal Communications Commission (1949, June 1). In the matter of editorializing by broadcast licensees, 13 FCC 1246.

Fleetwood, Blake (1999, September 1). The broken wall. *Washington Monthly,* 40.

Foisie, Geoffrey (1994, July 4). Harry and Louise: The sequel. *Broadcasting and Cable,* 39.

Gilje, Shelby (1995, August 2). Ad boycott catches FTC eye. *Seattle Times,* E1.

Giobe, Dorothy (1994, September 24). Ad director zaps columnist at his newspaper. *Editor & Publisher,* 26.

Grow, Doug (1991, November 29). Ads attacking NSP nuclear fuel rods storage plan didn't meet standards. *Minneapolis Star Tribune,* 3B.

Grow, Doug (1992, January 28). Column was too smart for Duluth newspaper. *Minneapolis Star Tribune,* 3B.

Hayward, Brad (1995, July 23). Hiding in the grass roots. *San Francisco Examiner,* B1.

Hays, Robert and Reisner, Ann (1990). Feeling the heat from advertisers: Farm magazine writers and ethical pressures. *Journalism Quarterly 67*, 938-941.

Higgins, Richard (1991, April 16). Ch. 7 is urged to release study on anti-Folgers ad. *Boston Globe,* 20.

Hough 3rd, George (1995). *News Writing, 5th ed.* Boston: Houghton Mifflin Co.

Howland, Jennifer (1989, December). Ad vs. edit: The pressure mounts. *Folio,* 952.

Kahn, Fred, ed. (1973). *Documents of American Broadcasting.* Englewood Cliffs, NJ: Prentice-Hall.

Knecht, G, Bruce (1997, April 30). Magazine advertisers demand prior notice of 'offensive' articles. *Wall Street Journal*, A1, A8.

Knecht, G. Bruce (1997a, October 22). Big retail chains get special advance look at magazine content. *Wall Street Journal,* A1, A13.

Krugman, Dean, Reid, Leonard, Dunn, H. Watson, and Barban, Arnold (1994). *Advertising, Its Role in Modern Marketing.* New York: The Dryden Press, 1994.

Kurtz, Howard (1994, July 21). Local stations bar ad attacking Pizza Hut. *Washington Post*, C1.

Kurtz, Howard (1996, December 16). 'Primetime' expose hits close to home. *Washington Post*, C1.

Laurence, Robert (1999, August 17). Sponsors' ties to content could bind TV. *San Diego Union-Tribune*, E6.

Lawrence, Donna (1995, July 17). Group questions dealer ad clout. *Automotive News,* 8.

Marcotty, Josephine (1992, March 28). Airline ads fly away. *Minneapolis Star Tribune*, 2D.

Miami Herald Publishing Co. v. Tornillo (1974) 418 U.S. 241.

Lesly, Elizabeth (1991, November). Realtors and builders demand happy news... and often get it. *Washington Journalism Review,* 21-23.

McInerney, Sally (1994, June 25). Tide turns fortunes of Edisto Beach newspaper. *Atlanta Journal and Constitution,* A3.

Mencher, Melvin (1986). *News Reporting and Writing.* Dubuque: Wm. C. Brown Publishers.

Milwaukee Journal Sentinel (1999, September 12 and September 19). Transportation section, 1.

Mink, Erik (1996, December 18). 'Primetime' looks at how big auto dealers steer local coverage. *New York Daily News,* 82,

Minneapolis Star Tribune (1991, November 30). Radio stations shy away from anti-Hudson ads, 2D.

Mores, Steve (1996, December 6). Up against the Wal-Mart. *Boston Globe,* C13.

Nauer, Kim and Rhodes, Steve (1992, March/April). Pottsville's 'better' paper. *Columbia Journalism Review,* 12-13.

Norris, Vincent (1982). Consumer magazine prices and the mythical advertising subsidy. *Journalism Quarterly 58,* 205-211, 239.

Ostrow, Joanne (2001, August 21). Sponsors dictate what's on the air. *Denver Post,* F5.

Palmer, Thomas (1990, May 17). Procter lays down the law on anti-Folgers ads. *Boston Globe,* 73.

Pergament, Alan (1996, February 21). Dropping of car leasing story backfires on Ch. 7's Cassidy. *Buffalo News,* 6.

Pew Research Center (1999). *Striking the Balance,* www.people-press.org/press99sec4.htm (accessed October 18, 2001).

Phillips, David (1997, October 14). Chrysler drops censorship policy. *Detroit News,* B11.

Pogrebin, Robert (1997, September 29). Magazine publishers circling wagons against advertising. *New York Times,* D1.

Ramirez, Anthony (1995, August 6). FTC slams car dealers on axed ads. *Houston Chronicle,* 5.

Robertson, Nan (1992). *The Girls in the Balcony.* New York: Random House, 1992.

Rosenberg, Neil (1999, August 3). Billboard firms take a pass on sexy ads. *Milwaukee Journal Sentinel*

Rotfeld, Herbert and Lacher, Kathleen (1994, January 3). Viewpoint: Advertisers have little say on news coverage. *Marketing News,* 4.

Rotfeld, Herbert and Lacher, Kathleen (1994a). Newspaper policies on the potential merging of advertising and news content. *Journal of Marketing and Public Policy 13,* 281-9.

Russell, J. Thomas and Lane, W. Ronald (1998). *Advertising Procedure, 14th ed.* Upper Saddle River, NJ: Prentice Hall.

San Francisco Chronicle (1996, November 18). Discounting lyrics to maximize sales, A24.

Santa Clara County v. Southern Pacific Railroad (1886), 118 U.S. 394.

Schoemer, Karen (1996, September 16). To her own self be true. *Newsweek*, 95.

Seaman, Debbie (1997, December 1). Hot potatoes: It's a safe bet that any TV station will air your Fab new detergent spot -- But what if your client is Planned Parenthood or a gay action group? *Creativity*, 32.

Seldes, George (1935). *Freedom of the Press.* New York: Bobbs-Merrill.

Sepinwall, Alan (2000, December 7). Cancelled TV show raises questions of advertiser influence. *Newhouse News Service.*

Shaw, David (1998, March 31). Breaching the wall. *Los Angeles Times*, A21.

Sherrill, Robert (1988, January). Big business takes the First. *Harper's*, 22.

Shone, Mark (1993, August 25). Advocacy ads rejected. *Inside Media*, 20.

Singer, Steve (1992, September). Auto dealers muscle the newsroom. *Washington Journalism Review*, 25-28.

Soley, Lawrence (1997, July/August). The power of the press has a price. *Extra!*, 11-13.

Soley, Lawrence and Craig, Robert L. (1992). Advertiser pressure on newspapers: A survey. *Journal of Advertising 21*, 1-10.

Standard Rate and Data Service (1999, April). *Newspaper Rates and Data*, 308.

Steinem, Gloria (1990, July/August). Sex, lies & advertising. *Ms.*, 18-28.

Stencel, Marc (1990, September 11). Boycotts a touchy business for targeted firms. *Los Angeles Times*, A2

Stewart, D. R.. (1996, September 12). Wal-Mart says customers understand ban on Crow CD. *Arkansas Democrat-Gazette*, 2D.

Swallow Williams, Wendy (1991, November). Two surveys show the industry's reach. *Washington Journalism Review,* 24.

Trigoboff, Dan (1999, June 7). Dealer ads motor from WXYZ-TV. *Broadcasting & Cable*, 27.

United Press International (1993, May 25). Anti-insurance ads banned in Boston. BC cycle.

Weisbaum, Herb (1990, Fall). Advertisers fight back. *IRE Journal*, 18.

Willis, Jim (1988). *Surviving in the Newspaper Business*. New York: Praeger.

Lawrence Soley is professor of journalism and the Colnik professor of communication at Marquette University in Milwaukee. Professor Soley's books include *Clandestine Radio Broadcasting* (with Johns S. Nichols), *Radio Warfare*, *The News Shapers*, *Leasing the Ivory Tower*, *Free Radio,* and *Censorship, Inc.* His research has appeared in a variety of scholarly journals, including *Journal of Communication*, *Journalism Quarterly*, *Newspaper Research Journal, Journal of Advertising* and *Journal of Public Policy and Marketing.*

Professor Soley's articles have also appeared in newspapers and magazines, including *Mother Jones*, *In These Times, Dollars and Sense, Dissent, Boston Phoenix*, and *Minneapolis City Pages*, for which he was a contributing writer.